Top 15 Secrets To Success In Business

Mark Cuban

The Sportsmanship Of Business

 EntrepreneurshipFacts.com

Warning-Disclaimer!

The purpose of this book is to educate and entertain. The author or publisher does not guarantee that anyone following the techniques, suggestions, tips, ideas, or strategies will become successful. The author and publisher shall have neither liability or responsibility to anyone with respect to any loss or damage caused or alleged to be caused, directly or indirectly by the information contained in this book.

All information contained within this book has been researched from reputable sources. If any information is found to be false, please contact the publisher, who will be happy to make corrections for future editions.

Follow EntrepreneurshipFacts on social media to stay updated with our free book promotions and increase your knowledge about business and successful people on a daily basis:

Instagram   Facebook   Twitter

Also check out our website for the latest facts and articles about business and entrepreneurship:

www.EntrepreneurshipFacts.com

Table of Contents

Introduction: 6

Short Biography 7

Lesson #1 - "Don't Drown In Opportunity" 16

Lesson #2 - "Failure is Part of the Success Equation" .. 22

Lesson #3 - "Gets Shit Done and Stays Productive" 26

Lesson #4 - "Money Can't Buy Happiness" 34

Lesson #5 - "The market could go up for years..." 38

Lesson #6 - "Treat your customers like they own you. Because they do." 44

Lesson #7 - "It's not in the dreaming, it's in the doing." 48

Lesson #8 - "The best startup capital is 'sweat equity'" 52

Lesson #9 - "Every rejection gets you closer to sales" . 59

Lesson #10 - "Find your weaknesses before competitors do" 64

Lesson #11 - "Be the best you can be." 67

Lesson #12 - *"Be optimistic from the moment you wake up"* 72

Lesson #13 - *"Everyone has ideas, most don't do the work required to get the job done."* 78

Lesson #14 - *"Do Something Different"* 84

Lesson #15 - *"Know Your Business Better than Anyone"* 90

Conclusion 97

Introduction:

Mark Cuban is an American businessman and investor. He is the owner of the NBA's Dallas Mavericks, Landmark Theatres, and Magnolia Pictures, and is the chairman of the HDTV cable network AXS TV. Cuban is also one of the main "shark" investors on the ABC reality television series, Shark Tank.

Throughout this book, we'll explore some of Mark Cuban's most famous quotes, taking a look at the context and significance of his statements. Following each is a summary of how these learnings can be applied to both business, and our daily lives.

Short Biography

Born to a middle-class family in Pittsburgh, Pennsylvania on July 31 of 1958, Mark Cuban's grandfather, Morris Chobanisky, was an immigrant from Russia and undoubtedly passed down values of hard work and a spirit of resiliancy and fortitude. After first coming to America, his grandfather made a living by selling a variety of items out of his truck, while Cuban's father worked at a upholstery shop for most of his career. Learning from his grandfather's entrepreneurial attitude, Cuban seemed to demonstrate a strong desire for crafting a better life, even at an early age. At the age of 12, he sold sets of garbage bags to save up for a pair of shoes he liked. Throughout his high school years, he did a number of jobs to earn extra cash, primarily selling stamps and coins.

His aptitude for sales and his ambitious demeanor served his success in school as well. Cuban began attending psychology at the University of Pittsburg while he was still a junior in high school. After getting a taste of university life, Cuban opted to forego his senior year and instead enrolled in full time college classes. Following his first year at the University of Pittsburgh, Cuban transferred to Indiana University, where his entrepreneurial streak continued. With the need to fund himself through school, he began offering dance lessons as a way to bolster his income. Shortly after, Cuban found himself playing host to disco parties at the Bloomingdale National Guard Armory.

Once he graduated, Cuban returned to Pittsburg and accepted a job with Mellon Bank. The organization was preparing to change to computers, and Cuban aptly decided to educate himself in the sector of machines and networking. He seemed to have a restless spirit, and after a short time in his hometown of Pittsburgh, he left the city, this time for Dallas.

His next job was selling software, which would eventually push him to create his very own business named MicroSolutions. Knowledgeable in computers and computer networking, he also had an innate business sense and an understanding of how to set up, manage and grow a successful company. By 1990, Cuban's company sold to CompuServe for an unprecedented $6 million.

Even after the sale of his company, Cuban had a desire for more. The Internet had captivated the world and pushed the boundaries of what was possible, and Cuban sensed it was the perfect time for a new project. He had a friend from Indiana University, Todd Wagner, and in 1995, the two launched AudioNet. The primary driver of AudioNet was to move the commentary about the Indiana Hoosier basketball games online. While many people criticized the concept, it was extremely successful. Cuban and Wagner renamed the company to Broadcast.com, and after going public in 1998, soon reached an impressive $200 per share. Only a year after, the two of them would sell the company to Yahoo! for almost $6 billion.

In the year 2000, Cuban entered the world of sports, purchasing the Dallas Mavericks for $285 million. Cuban was a long-standing ticket holder, he was excited to play a bigger role in the sports sector. This decision, however, would turn out to be much different than he anticipated.

As numerous poor decisions had been made in the past, and a number of coaches and players that failed to fulfill expectations, the club had gone over 10 years without making the playoffs. As a new owner, Cuban tried immediately to turn things around. With a spirit of excitement and tenacity, he began to spur cultural changes within the team, created a new stadium and worked to instill a sense of pride in the team's players. During this time, Cuban successfully carved out his reputation for being the club's biggest fan. Sitting in the stands along with the crowd, Cuban cheered and booed with everyone else, and the Mavericks greatly appreciated his seemingly endless enthusiasm.

The team, perhaps with a renewed enthusiasm, reached the playoffs in 2001, and surpassed the previously existing franchise record, achieving an incredible 57 wins the next year. In 2006, the Mavericks reached the NBA Finals before a devastating loss to the Miami Heat. However, in 2011, they would achieve redemption and defeat the Heat for the NBA title.

In addition to his enthusiasm, Cuban had an innovative and unique approach that benefited the team. Creating a blog, he discussed both his insights on the tech world and his personal viewpoints on the NBA. The blog took the world by storm. It was the first of its kind, and Cuban was soon receiving thousands of messages per day from eager fans and daily readers.

As the most renowned and wealthy investor on Shark Tank, Cuban is part of a panel referred to as the "Sharks". A variety of entrepreneurs from different sectors come to the show to pitch investors. While Cuban first appeared on the show as a guest in its second season, he went on to become a regular on the investor panel. With a net worth of $3.3 billion (2016), Mark Cuban's personal net worth is greater than all of the other Sharks who have appeared on the TV show Shark Tank.

As of January 2016, Cuban has said "yes" to 82 deals and invested $19.4 million via *Shark Tank* episodes. Because due diligence is conducted after the initial "handshake" on television occurs, these numbers may be slightly different due to occasional deals falling through. For example, Cuban agreed to a $1.25 million deal for a 100% stake in the company Hy-Conn, which manufactures fire hoses--however, this didn't end up working out. While Cuban agreed to a number of high budget deals, his largest included Ten Thirty One Productions, Rugged Maniac Obstacle Race, and BeatBox Beverages.

In spite of Cuban's already evident success, he has continued to press on. Testing the waters in the TV market, he developed HDNet, which would go on to be known as AXS TV. Some are aware Cuban created his own reality television series, and even came on *Dancing with the Stars* as a contestant in 2007, upon the counsel of his daughter.

Purchasing the well-known movie chains Landmark Theatres and Magnolia Pictures, Cuban has also found his name among the credits in movies such as *Goodnight and Good Luck* and

Akeelah and the Bee. His various television appearances include features on *Entourage* and *The League.* Even in 2015, Cuban starred on the movie version of *Entourage* as well as in *Sharknado 3* where his movie role was President of the United States.

Cuban has always been a constant in the world of professional athletics. When Alex Rodriguez was suspended for 211 games in 2013 for alleged use of performance-enhancing drugs, Cuban became an advocate and called attention to the heavy-handed sentence. Normally, first-time offenders receive a suspension for 50 games, and 100 games for a second incident. Consequently, Rodriguez' ban seemed extremely harsh, and Cuban didn't back down, going as far as to appear on the *Tonight Show* and call the suspension "personal". Cuban then stirred up additional controversy about the industry in general, claiming he would never choose to purchase a baseball team as he felt that Bud Selig, the current MLB Commissioner, ran the sport like a "mafia".

In 2014, Cuban launched an app called Cyber Dust, demonstrating he still had a strong presence in the tech sector. In 2015, he received national attention again during he U.S. presidential campaign, claiming he could win against both Hillary Clinton and Donald Trump for the presidential spot. Following such an outrageous claim, he ultimately backed Hillary Clinton in July 2016.

Now that you have learned a bit about his background, here are 15 life and business lessons can be learned from billionaire Mark Cuban.

Quote #1

"Don't Drown In Opportunity"

Quote Meaning

According to Mark Cuban, "If you are adding new things when your core businesses are struggling rather than facing the challenge, you are either running away or giving up. Rarely is either good for a business."

A number of years ago, Cuban made a deal on *Shark Tank* with a woman named Melissa Carbone, President of *Ten Thirty One Productions*, a horror attraction company. After the show aired, Carbone was overwhelmed with deals and offers to invest in her company, many of which were incredibly tempting. At the time, Cuban advised her to relax, refocus and not make any impulsive decisions.

According to Carbone, his advice, "Don't drown in opportunity," resonated with her for years to come.

Cuban's underlying belief is to ensure that you are winning the battles you are in before taking on new battles.

"Every one of my businesses has a make or breaks battle going on and so do yours. There is one battle in your business that you are not winning, or are battling to stay in front. In our film business, it's the battle to get people to theaters without spending more than we bring in box office. With the Mavs, it's the battle of making our game experience in the arena and on TV so compelling that its strong enough entertainment on its own to draw an audience and make our advertisers happy. I can't control how a game on the court goes, but I can make sure that if you come to, or watch a game you have a great time doing it. On HDNet, it's how to keep on raising the bar and find or create programming that our subscribers feel committed to and take ownership of. I can spend as much money on a show as a big network, but they are wrong 95% of the time. It's not a model I want to copy. It's the ultimate challenge to find a new way to get results."

For example, at one point, Cuban faced the option to go global with Landmark Theatres. However, he also realized that the work required to focus on breaking into the international market would take away from his focus nationally. Consequently, he opted not to expand.

"You do not have unlimited time and/or attention," he writes. "You may work 24 hours a day, but those 24 hours spent winning your core business will pay off far more. It might cost you some longer-term upside, but it will allow you to be the best business you can be."

It's often tempting to move on to the next project before the first one has finished successfully. However, taking a lesson from the pages of

Cuban's book can be valuable; instead of heading into the next challenge, we need to push ourselves to wrap up the challenges we're already working on. Of course, the latest shiny object is exciting, and it's much easier to move on instead of having the willpower to follow through on our current projects, but that doesn't matter. Eventually, the novelty will wear off and "the latest" thing will be just as hard to finish as the challenges that came before. Again, its completion will seem far away and other projects will capture our attention. However, giving in to this trend of jumping to the next thing that intrigues us will leave us with an endless list of half-completed projects and hardly any accomplishments.

Whenever your attention is being drawn by the excitement of the "next big thing," take the time to consider your goals, and what you ultimately want to accomplish. Remind yourself that at one point, the project you're currently working on seemed equally enthralling.

By realizing what's happening when these situations occur, you will quickly learn that often, the grass isn't greener on the other side, but is merely an intriguing distraction that will cause you to lose focus. When the project you're working on begins to feel mundane, it is our natural instinct to be drawn away by new ideas and the excitement of the unknown--this is why the tendency to procrastinate is a tough challenge to overcome.

Finishing what you've begun will undoubtedly make you feel better than simply getting started on a new project. By refusing to lose focus and recognize that the "latest thing" is often simply a distraction from your boredom, you're already a step ahead.

Business Lesson

Regardless of the sector, business owners and entrepreneurs have a keen business sense and are always vulnerable to the lure of a new project or an exciting collaboration. While this is a great thing, it also needs to be approached with caution. By allowing yourself to "drown" in all the opportunities you are faced with, you may end up failing at all of them. Instead, by slowing down and refusing to take on the next challenge until you finish current projects, success is much more likely. Ensure the right resources and processes are in place, and that things can run smoothly without the attention you will undoubtedly have to divert to a new project. By making sure you follow your current projects right through to the end, you'll undoubtedly be successful and get the profit you need to start your next project off on the right foot.

Quote #2

"Failure is Part of the Success Equation"

Quote Meaning

While Mark Cuban's many successes are evident, he has also admitted to multiple failures throughout his life, as he described in a candid interview with *Entrepreneur* magazine. He recounted his attempt at selling powdered milk, which ultimately ended in failure. Expecting quick success in his business, it didn't take long for him to realize this was a venture that wasn't going to succeed. "I honestly thought it would make a killer business and it lasted minutes," he says. Cuban also claims that he's been fired from "more jobs than most people have had." In addition, he's experienced a number of failings as an entrepreneur. He talks about numerous deals he was unable to close, or having his credit card repeatedly declined--one time even cut up.

Despite these numerous instances of failure, Cuban refused to give up on the dreams of success that first began in his childhood, selling garbage bags to pay for a coveted pair of sneakers. Rather, Cuban remains grateful for the twists and turns he's faced on his long and unpredictable journey to success. "It doesn't matter how many times you fail. Each time only makes you better, stronger, smarter and you only have to be right once. Just once," he says. "Then everyone calls you an overnight success and you feel lucky. I still feel that way."

Cuban's ultimate success is undeniable. Making a few million from the sale of his consulting company to CompuServe, he's grown his net worth to an estimated $3.3 billion dollars (2016). With an amount that would be almost impossible to spend, Cuban continues to seek new opportunities and invest in more projects.

"I wouldn't be where I am now if I didn't fail... a lot. The good, the bad, it's all part of the success equation. I really wouldn't change anything at all."

Business Lesson

Failure is undoubtedly one of mankind's greatest fears. However, the fact remains that each one of us has failed, and we will all fail again at some point. It's easy to see the successes of famous and wealthy individuals such as Cuban, and forget about the times they didn't succeed. The difference is, successful people refuse to give in to failure. Standing up and trying again, they refuse to let setbacks define them. Instead, outstanding entrepreneurs arm themselves with the resiliency and fortitude needed to surpass the bumps in the road and press on towards achievement. Rather than giving in to disappointing situations or inevitable failures, they focus on the end goal and keep going.

As a society, we have a tendency to assume that people who succeed do so because of something that was given to them, or chalk it up to them being in the right place at the right time. However, we often gloss over their repeated failures and ignore the countless times they got back up and tried again. We zero in on the positive, and discount the years they have spent struggling and facing adversity. While these hardships may not be the first thing we take note of, surpassing obstacles and overcoming challenges is the most inspiring and motivational part of an individual's story. Rather than being afraid of failing, embrace it. It is a key part of the journey and an essential element in forging your path to success.

Quote #3

"Gets Shit Done and Stays Productive"

Quote Meaning

Over time, Mark Cuban has invested in more than 100 companies. He is married with three children, and owner of a professional basketball team. Evidently, Cuban hasn't risen to where he is by living a life of mediocrity. Instead, the entrepreneurial mindset he had since childhood has pushed him to work his way to the top, from an employee learning the ropes to an accomplished billionaire.

Mark Cuban once described himself on the *Shark Tank* show as a person who "gets shit done," and this becomes evident when looking at his long list of accomplishments. Cuban no doubt has hired a variety of staff to help him with everything from childcare to running errands, but he still remains in control of his day. One thing that Cuban has always credited as a key factor in staying productive is having phone calls and meetings only when necessary.

"I don't like to do a lot of meetings and phone calls because of the productivity hit," he tells *Entrepreneur Magazine*. "Only if you're writing me a check, I'll do a meeting. If there's a problem and we need to solve it, I'll do a call. Other than that, I keep communication limited to email. It's more efficient."

In order to stay focused and make the most of his talent, experience and time, he zeroes in on the urgent. "With my investments, I want the bad news first by email, and if it's bad, I'll jump on that," he says. "For the good, well, that's what I expect. That's why I invest in you. I don't spend time on good news because there's nothing to fix."

Business Lesson

Regardless of your profession or focus, productivity is an important part of life. However, drinking coffee and making "to-do" lists isn't necessarily going to bolster our productivity. Why is being productive so important? In today's era, keeping focused and avoiding the millions of distractions vying for our attention can be harder than ever. In addition, knowing we've had a highly productive day can be a great feeling.

However, in our quest for productivity, there have been many myths we've come to accept along the way. Instead of simply accomplishing tasks, the world's most productive individuals focus on having *fewer* things on their to-do list, and ensure they do these well. You too can achieve a high standard of productivity by focusing on the following:

1. **Do Less**. A productive day at work doesn't always mean that you've checked off a mile-long list. Instead, revisit the items you have planned and objectively assess what's important. Then, take a highly focused approach and tackle the most important tasks.

2. **Take a Moment.** Often, we'll get a feeling of fatigue after being in the zone for a few hours. Take note of your body's signals and allow yourself to take a break. Head out for a quick jog, have a bite to eat, or simply take a few moments to breathe and reset. Instead of forging on in an unproductive state, you'll be able to restart your work with a renewed sense of focus.

3. **Use the 80/20 Rule.** The 80/20 Rule states that the 20% of our work actually drives 80% of the results we achieve. However, we often focus on accomplishing tasks that are hardly making a difference to our outcomes. Consider reevaluating what you're working on and distilling out the tasks

that are actually driving the results. Then, focus on these things.

4. Take some "me" time in the morning. Many of us will begin checking our emails, messages and schedule first thing in the morning; however, this can be a huge time waster. In addition, it's letting others drive our schedule. Get the day off to a great start by avoiding emails until you have something to eat, browse through the morning's news, take a few moments to mediate, or visit the gym for a quick workout. By allowing some time for yourself before anything, you'll be in the right frame of mind for a truly successful day.

5. Accomplish some big-ticket items before lunch. Try to tackle some of the bigger tasks on your to-do list in the morning before you hit that afternoon slump. If you have less complex tasks or a business meeting, consider pushing them off to the afternoon. By organizing your time like this, you'll be able to enjoy a strong sense of productivity and a different approach to time management.

6. Reconsider your approach to email. Reviewing endless emails and answering them immediately can zap your productivity like nothing else. Don't let yourself get sucked in by common behaviors that are lazy and inefficient. One thing to avoid is copying individuals that don't need to be included on emails. While it may be the easy way of getting an email off your radar, it distracts others and can be overwhelming to people receiving endless messages that don't involve them. Instead, after receiving an email with numerous people cc'd, consider bcc'ing these people in your reply. And, if it's taking you more than a couple messages to deal with the issue, get on the phone so you can wrap things up quickly.

7. Define your approach. Like most of us, it's likely that you've picked up a few negative habits when it comes to productivity. Being aware of these behaviors and creating a system to manage them can be key in tackling your productivity challenges. If you find it hard to resist checking email, decide on certain times of day you will check it. By taking a systems approach, you'll avoid distraction and add significantly more focus to your day.

8. Make sure "time-saving" tactics are actually productive. Although it's hard to admit to, being lazy is a key factor that holds us back from being productive. For example, things we've always thought of as "convenient," such as sending an email or booking a meeting, can actually distract us from accomplishing what we need to. Instead, zero in on the tasks that are most important, and how to get these done quickly and efficiently.

9. Stop trying to multi-task. Multi-tasking can be a productivity killer. In fact, it's been said that switching activities over 10 times within the workday effectively decreases your IQ by 10 points. Instead, add a dose of efficiency by finishing one thing at a time and refusing to get distracted by other tasks. When it comes to productivity, it's better to focus on doing a few things well than doing many things poorly.

Quote #4

"Money Can't Buy Happiness"

Quote Meaning

As a society, we often ask ourselves if money can truly buy happiness. According to Cuban, it most certainly won't.

"Can money buy happiness?" Cuban was asked between pitches on the *Shark Tank* set. "Absolutely not," he replied, without hesitation. "To me, success isn't defined by your wallet. It's defined by waking up with a smile on your face, knowing it's going to be a great day. But, sure, money can make your life a whole lot easier."

Mark Cuban undoubtedly enjoys the luxuries of a wealthy life due to his early success in selling his companies to the likes of CompuServe and Yahoo.

Purchases such as the $285 million Dallas Mavericks, a private jet, or a huge mansion in his upscale Dallas neighborhood are beyond what most people could ever dream of purchasing. After the Mavericks won their first NBA championship game, the team racked up a $90,000 tab at the bar celebrating, which Cuban picked up. However, Cuban has always claimed that his financial wealth or a luxurious existence isn't the driving force to his happiness. "It's creating a goal for yourself and accomplishing a goal and setting a dream, and living that dream through your effort that can make you feel a whole lot better about yourself," he says. "It worked for me. So, while money can't buy happiness, it can sure make life a whole lot better." This definitely makes a lot of sense.

Business Lesson

There are endless hang-ups people seem to have about finances. Without money, we often feel that more of it would make us happy. When money is plentiful, we may focus on what we could have with "more" money. While our logic tells us that money doesn't buy happiness, our emotions may tell us otherwise. The lure of upscale cars, bigger houses and luxury travel make us believe that happiness can be achieved through material goods. However, the fact remains that money isn't the key to our happiness.

While all the things in the world can't make us happy, it doesn't mean the opposite rings true. A life without money, and continuously feeling deprived, isn't a lot of fun either. The presence of money, material possessions or working long hours at work isn't innately wrong. We all need to support ourselves, and money is a non-negotiable part of our existence. However, when we focus on financial wealth and material goods above all, we fail to put our true priorities first, and the things that give our lives purpose.

Consequently, minimizing some of the unnecessary "stuff" in our lives can not only save our money and sanity, but provide us with the mind space to refocus on what's important: our health, the people we care about, personal growth, contributing to society, and developing our communities. While financial success can provide us with the luxury to excel in some of these areas, the number in the bank account becomes significantly less of an issue when we align our day-to-day priorities with our underlying values.

Quote #5

"The market could go up for years, and you could think you're well off, and then, in a millisecond with high-frequency trading, a flash crash can take it all away. That's why you want to have that money in the mattress, that savings, so you're protected in case something goes wrong."

Quote Meaning

Mark Cuban has a reputation for saying exactly what he thinks. When being asked for his best advice to make money investing. His reply was, "don't."

"The market could go up for years, and you could think you're well off," he said, "and then, in a millisecond with high-frequency trading, a flash crash can take it all away. That's why you want to have that money in the mattress, that savings, so you're protected in case something goes wrong."

His reference to the "money in the mattress" is Cuban's repeated advice for everyone to have a six-month savings fund available in case of an emergency. "I know it doesn't earn much in the bank, but you'll sleep a lot better."

Many people will notice a disconnect between the advice that Cuban offers about investing and that given by the majority of financial professionals. Generally, most people are not advised to take on unnecessary risk and attempt to "beat the market," and will instead be warned to open retirement savings accounts and keep their money growing throughout the years. Some of the world's most wealthy individuals--Warren Buffett, Charles

Schwab or Charlie Munger--will tout low-cost index funds as a great option for the average investor.

"A low-cost index fund is the most sensible equity investment for the great majority of investors," Buffett told Bogle in *The Little Book of Common Sense Investing*. "By periodically investing in an index fund, the know-nothing investor can actually outperform most investment professionals."

Some people may choose to put extra money into investments, while others will opt for establishing a bigger savings account. Regardless, ensuring you have a six-month emergency fund at a minimum will help you rest easy that you'll be covered should something unexpected happen. Evidently, not all of Cuban's financial advise is echoed by financial professionals, but the emergency fund is a goal that seems to be agreed on by everyone.

Business Lesson

Saving money wisely can propel you towards financial security and give you a safety net should something unexpected happen in your life. Your house suddenly needing a new roof, an unexpected medical bill, or losing your job can quickly impact your financial situation, and having a savings fund can cushion you from an otherwise drastic fall.

For those with a modest income who are barely making ends meet, the concept of diverting extra money to a savings fund might seem unimaginable. If you're left with hardly anything after paying your bills, it can seem impossible to start saving. However, by starting small and focusing on what you *can* do, you can improve your situation steadily over time. Saving money, no matter how modestly, can allow you to reap big benefits. It will decrease your stress, knowing you have a safety net to fall back on; it can give you more flexibility in making life decisions, and as your savings grow, you'll find it increasingly easy to save more.

By growing your savings and having the willpower to live within your means, you will give yourself a greater sense of peace. You'll know your mortgage is covered even if your paycheck is delayed. You'll have the financial freedom to be selective about your next job rather than accepting the first thing that comes along. Or, perhaps you'll have the option of sending your kids to that new school. Whatever your priorities, you'll be much more at peace knowing your finances are under control, and you'll have the mental space to focus your attention on other facets of your life.

Quote #6

"Treat your customers like they own you. Because they do."

Quote Meaning

Regardless of the size of your enterprise, Cuban would tell you that you never truly own it. Instead, your clients are effectively the owners of your company. "It is so much easier to be nice, to be respectful, to put yourself in your customers' shoes and try to understand how you might help them before they ask for help, than it is to try to mend a broken customer relationship," Cuban says.

In today's age, an unsatisfied customer can share their negative experience easier than ever before, whether on social media or reviewing your site online. More than ever, it's essential to craft a great experience for your clients and commit to working issues out quickly before a situation escalates.

Having a client-focused approach is essential to success in business. Having a great customer experience can allow you to stand out amongst your peers--in fact, research shows that most organizations are failing when it comes to this experience:

Only 37% of brands received good or excellent customer experience index scores in 2012. An entire 64% of brands got a rating of "OK," "poor," or "very poor" from their customers (Source: Forrester Research).

As many as 89% of consumers began doing business with a competitor following a poor customer experience (Source: RightNow).

Up to 60% of consumers will pay more for a better customer experience (Source: Desk).

Average annual value of each customer relationship lost to a competitor or abandoned – $289 (Source: Genesys Report).

It's quite evident that creating a strong customer experience and a positive working relationship is essential to success. And, accomplishing this falls back to creating an environment of trust and support. Cuban's quote reiterates the fact that a business cannot be successful without its customers. By refusing to take customers for granted and reminding ourselves that these people are driving the success of our company, we can forge stronger customer relationships.

One major key to keeping clients happy and satisfied is being accessible. "In every business I have had, I have made sure my customers have had my email address and can reach me directly," Cuban says. "I've given my email address out on national TV. Customers of any of our businesses can and do email me with questions and comments. Each and every email is an opportunity for me to solidify a customer relationship or to add a new customer. I'm shocked that more entrepreneurs don't do the same."

Business Lesson

As a business owner, we can take our clients for granted and forget that our customers are paying our bills. There are many reasons why a person chooses to support our company. They may believe that the products we sell or services offered are high caliber. It may be that they personally support us. Regardless, clients have to be treated with unparalleled respect and consideration. Creating strong and professional relationships with customers is a key factor in the success of any company. And, in this age of technology, automation and convenience, creating a strong and effective relationship is more important than ever before.

Quote #7

"It's not in the dreaming, it's in the doing."

Quote Meaning

Most of us have been told how important it is to "dream big." We are often told that to be successful in our lives or our businesses, we need to envision success and picture the outcome before it happens. While dreaming may help us clarify our priorities or paint an exciting vision for the future, we know that simply dreaming about something will not guarantee it happens. Any goal or vision has to be followed up by action and effort. And, there's a big difference between thinking about something happening, and going through the steps to make it happen.

Cuban has stated that prior to his success in business, he would drive past large houses every weekend and wonder who lived there. He would wonder what they did to make a living, or how they brought in their money. He would tell himself that someday, he would live in a house like that. What separated Cuban from others was his commitment to riding out the rough patches, overcoming obstacles and pressing on to his goal in order to eventually earn the money to purchase a home of that caliber. Coming to this realization is pivotal for an entrepreneur. By staying focused and being committed to the journey, we can turn a dream into reality. However, without a willingness to put in the effort and make things happen, our dreams will remain unfulfilled.

Business Lesson

Throughout our lives, we are advised that anything is possible, and dreaming big is encouraged. However, this advice is often not accompanied by the realization that we must work hard to accomplish what we envision. Dreams are great, but following through on the steps needed to accomplish them, and taking action, is where the true impact is. If your dream is to become a medical doctor, take the prerequisites required, apply for medical school and continue along the journey. If your dream is to become a politician, start getting involved with local initiatives, or connect with a political mentor and begin learning the ropes. Whatever our dreams, they need to be accompanied by actions to transition them to reality. If dreams are never followed up by appropriate steps, they will never be accomplished. If we want to reach our dreams, we must put in a valiant effort to start down the path towards them. Although our time, money or resources may be limited at the time, there is always something that can be done to start moving towards the goal, rather than treading water.

Each person has a unique set of skills and talents, and their own dream for the future. Knowing this, we need to forego our excuses and focus on taking the actions needed to reach these goals, even when faced with adversity.

The legwork needed to accomplish a dream may seem overwhelming sometime, but it's important to remember that every huge accomplishment can be divided up into small steps and daily actions. By taking things a step at a time, and always ensuring you're moving closer, rather than further away from your goal, eventually you will get there. Rather than focus on the size of your dream, focus on inching closer each day. With this approach, you'll be able to look back over time and see truly how far you've come.

Quote #8

"The best startup capital is 'sweat equity"

Quote Meaning

The time and effort that is given to a project is often referred to as *sweat equity*. Rather than a financial investment, it is the energy that has been put into developing a startup company, a project or initiative. Sweat equity can come from the company's founders, advisors or even board members.

In some cases, some people may choose to contribute financially, whereas others invest their time and energy. Consequently, partnerships such as these are a mix of financial investment and sweat equity. In the end, this effort is valued much the same as money would be, by distributing stock or similar equity forms.

Another form of sweat equity can be energy invested into any type of project. A homeowner who has spent hours to repair, renovate and fix up their residence may be effectively adding value to their home.

In the world of business, Cuban believes that individuals should never be defeated by a lack of funding or not having the right connections. "Great entrepreneurs invest the time, no matter how many hours a day, to learn more about their industry and the business they want to start than anyone else," he says. "They realize that ramen noodles and macaroni and cheese are the fuel they need because every other penny they get from working that night job is going to fund their business."

Cuban is well aware of the amount of sacrifice it can take to develop a successful business. "When I started MicroSolutions, I had just been fired from my last job and was living in a three-bedroom apartment with five other guys," he recalls. "I slept on the floor. My dinner was usually the late chicken dinner at Tom Thumb for $1.29...it allowed me to stay focused on turning MicroSolutions into a $30 million business."

According to Cuban, "The best businesses in recent entrepreneurial history are those that have been started with little or no money. Dell Computer, MicroSoft, Apple, HP and tens of thousands of others started in dorm rooms, tiny offices or garages. There weren't 100 page long business plans. In all of my businesses, I started by putting together spreadsheets of my expenses, which allowed me to calculate how much revenue I needed to break even and keep the lights on in my office and my apartment. I wrote overviews of what I was selling, why I thought the business made sense, an overview of my competition and why my product and/or service would be important to my customers, and why they should buy or use it. All of it on a piece of yellow paper or in a word processing file, and none of it cost me more than the diet soda I was drinking while I was writing it up."

Business Lesson

For a new company, sweat equity can be a huge positive. It can allow the organization to save money that would otherwise have to be spent on salaries, advertising, or overhead costs. For those who are looking to invest in your company, sweat equity can be seen as a huge positive, as it indicates the loyalty and commitment exhibited by its founders. If partners are willing to work with a minimal salary and invest their own sweat equity, it shows they truly believe the company can be successful. Having a stake in the company is valuable to them, as they believe when the company is successful, they will then be able to benefit.

The owner of a business should have a strong understanding of how to value sweat equity. Before giving someone's sweat equity a specific value, you should assess partners, colleagues or staff for the following traits:

Commitment: Do they exhibit a strong commitment to being a founding partner for your business?

Unique Contribution: Do these people bring knowledge, skills, leadership ability or previous experience to the table that you can't?

Alignment of Values: Are their values pertaining to wealth, success and work ethic the same as yours? If not, are the differences major enough that they could cause division down the road?

When you lack the proper funding or capital to grow your business, sweat equity can be a huge benefit. As a business owner, consider negotiating an agreement with shareholders where you can exchange a high salary for equity in the company, perhaps providing them the option to buy shares at a discounted rate or increasing their ownership percentage based on high performance.

What you lack in initial capital, you can offset with your time, energy and contributions. Often, this approach can give your company the resources it needs to take off, while allowing you to maintain some level of control over future profits and ownership.

Sweat equity is a fantastic concept when you have the ability to dedicate significant energy into getting a business off the ground, and allows you to share the workload with your employees and partners. Dedication and sacrifices upfront can help you achieve long term success in your venture.

Quote #9

"Every rejection gets you closer to sales"

Quote Meaning

Although Cuban was already worth billions in his early 40s, he faced a lot of challenges and difficulties along the way. "I worked jobs I didn't like," Cuban states. "I worked jobs I loved, but had no chance of being a career. I worked jobs that barely paid the rent. I had so many jobs my parents wondered if I would be stable."

From selling garbage bags to pay for shoes, to unsuccessfully selling powdered milk, Cuban faced a lot of adversity in the early part of his career. Being cut from his high school basketball team, or having his credit card declined, he could hardly have been blamed for losing hope of being successful. However, Cuban remained optimistic. "I was just hoping the confidence would win over the doubt and it would all work out for the best." he said.

Cuban always retained his childhood dream of launching a business. While he faced numerous failures, he always remembered it only took one time for his business to take off. As Cuban has explained, "Rejection has only been a distraction, not a roadblock. Every 'no' gets me closer to a 'yes,' was the saying I used to use."

Rather than giving in to his failures, Cuban took each obstacle in stride and tried to learn from it. "I'm the type that thinks if you don't learn from history, you're doomed to repeat it," he claims. "With every effort, I learned a lot. With every mistake and failure, not only mine, but of those around me, I learned what not to do." By analyzing the numerous successes and frequent failures his friends, family and colleagues experienced, he was able to soak up lessons from almost anywhere.

"I had more than a healthy dose of fear, and an unlimited amount of hope, and more importantly, no limit on time and effort." Cuban didn't focus on the amount of ventures that didn't work out. Instead, he remained confident that once he figured things out, his past failures would be forgotten, and people would begin to focus on his success. "It doesn't matter how many times you fail," Cuban says. "It doesn't matter how many times you almost get it right. No one is going to know or care about your failures, and neither should you. All you have to do is learn from them and those around you."

Evidently, Cuban had a strong understanding that an entrepreneur's life is full of trials, risks and uncertainty, but with the potential to pay off tenfold. "All that matters in business is that you get it right once," he states. "Then everyone can tell you how lucky you are."

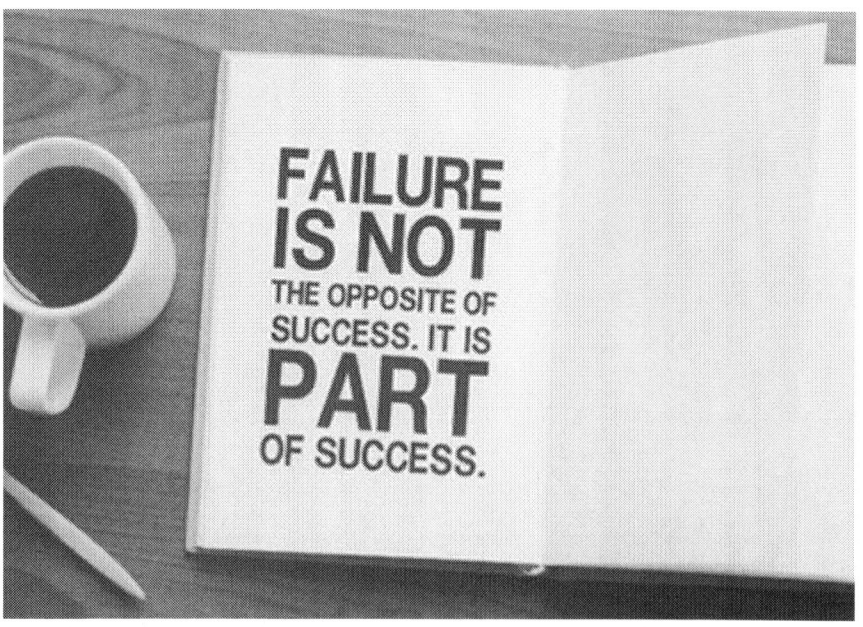

Business Lesson

Rather than fearing rejection or failure, business owners should embrace it. A prime example is Thomas Edison, who viewed each unsuccessful attempt at creating the light bulb as a way to learn more about how to succeed. Instead of focusing on the failure, he saw it as another pathway he could cast aside in favor of trying something else. Taking this approach, each failure brings us closer to success, telling us to try something different. No matter what goals have been set, we will not be able to accomplish them if we allow failures to disappoint us and set us back. Each rejection, each obstacle and each delay helps bring us closer to figuring out a better way to attain our goal.

As a business owner, it's wise to look at each failure as exactly what it is: an opportunity to learn, and a helpful step on the way to reaching a goal.

Quote #10

"Find your weaknesses before competitors do"

Quote Meaning

Sharing your idea with the world is one thing, but as Cuban will advise, in order to be successful, you also have to be well ahead of the competitors that are vying for your place in the market.

"If you have a business that competes with one of mine, I am going to try to kick your --- and put you out of business," he claims. "I presume that you are trying to do the same thing [to me]…which is why I always try to look at each of my businesses from the perspective of my competition. I think, 'If I wanted to put my company out of business, what would I do? If I wanted to take customers away, what would I, as a competitor, do?' "

The majority of the time, this can be done by honing in on what your competitor does poorly, or identifying any deficiencies in their product or service. However, it's simply good business sense to take the time to analyze and assess your rivals.

It will also benefit any business owner to keep in mind that rivals are doing the same thing; comparing their product to yours, zeroing in on your weak points rather than your strengths. Consequently, you can get a few steps ahead by being brutally honest with yourself and addressing any weaknesses before your competitor is able to. Pour over the complaints you've received and identify any opportunities for improvement; reassess your internal processes to look for operational inefficiencies. Ask your client-facing staff if they have any recommendations for improvement, or if they are aware of issues with the product or service. Consider what you can do to address any of these weaknesses ahead of time.

Business Lesson

No organization is perfect, but as the company's owner, it's up to you to identify weaknesses and take care of them before your competitors are able to discover them. By looking at your business objectively, you can be realistic about flaws and identify areas for improvement. Consider the level of customer satisfaction or opportunities for improved communication; assess the relationship you have with vendors or suppliers and determine whether there are areas to grow. Consider any skills, expertise or experience that your team lacks, and think about ways to fill these roles or grow the capacity of your people. By looking at your business operations objectively, you can do a better job of understanding your weak points and effectively tackling them before your competition is able to use them against you.

Quote #11

"Be the best you can be."

Quote Meaning

When you know your passion in life, Cuban believes the next step is "to be the best in the world at it."

This statement is far from empty. Cuban feels that you must give 100% effort to being great at your job, and continuously look for ways to improve. Through this approach, you'll stand out from the crowd and generate a reputation for being the best at what you do. In fact, Cuban advocates you'll know you're successful when demand for your services increases. "Rather than trying to convince people you are the best, let the quality of your work do the talking." Cuban writes.

Instead of comparing yourself to others or focusing on the steps needed to become "great," happy and successful people simply focus on being genuine and continuously improving. Rather than trying to fulfill a certain brand or live up to a specific persona, they focus on being the best version of themselves.

There is definitely no easy path to success, and becoming an expert in your field will undoubtedly take a substantial effort. However, pushing the boundaries and taking calculated risks is key to any accomplishment.

Business Lesson:

While we will undoubtedly face times of frustration, anxiety or disappointment, we all have a unique skill set. While it may not be evident at first glance, our specific talents, abilities and passions can help us in accomplishing what we're meant to do.

The following advice can help you focus on becoming the best you can be:

Find your purpose. Perhaps you have a certain talent or passion you would like to develop. If not, you are likely aware of what you want to experience in life - to be happier, to improve communication with friends or family, or to find more fulfillment in your job. Being aware of your purpose is important, as it allows you a baseline from which to base everyday decisions.

Live intentionally. Each day, ensure that you are making decisions with intention. Keeping in mind the type of life you want to live, ensure that the choices you make and the things you allow in your life are consistent with your vision.

Put your passion into action. If you have a certain skill, ability or talent, don't let it fade into the background. Putting your passion into action is a surprisingly simple concept. If you would like to be happier, do things that make you happy. If you want to refine a talent you have, make sure you are open to learning and improvement. If you enjoy public speaking, find opportunities to nurture this skill.

Live in the moment. Rather than only focusing on where you want to be, be grateful for the "now". Notice the blessings you have in your life. Don't take yourself too seriously and learn to laugh at your mistakes and move on. On a daily basis, think about what you want to achieve and how you will do it. Stay open and ready for opportunities that may present themselves unexpectedly.

Build your support network. Ensure you surround yourself by people who support you in achieving your vision. Learn from others and allow yourself to grow, surrounding yourself with people who push themselves in the same way you do.

Minimize the clutter. Don't be afraid to get rid of what is no longer serving you. By living a "lean" lifestyle, you'll have a more stress-free life and enjoy the feeling that comes with having less.

Stay focused. We all have limited hours in a day. Using your values and goals as a filter, deal with the daily issues that crop up without letting them throw you off course. Be realistic about what you agree to take on, and learn to say "no" to opportunities that don't bring you closer to your goals.

Prioritize yourself. Each day, take actions that allow you to function at your best. Eating healthier, drinking more water, getting enough sleep and regular exercise will help serve you in the long run. By ensuring health and wellness is always a priority, you're investing in yourself and improving your ability to accomplish more.

Quote #12

"Be optimistic from the moment you wake up"

Quote Meaning

Cuban is realistic about failure. "You are going to screw up," he writes. "We all do. I can't tell you how many times I did and continue to."

However, it's also important to let go of these failures and view them simply as a way to learn. While everyone undoubtedly will feel negative emotions--anger, frustration, and disappointment--it's important to move on rather than wallowing in these feelings of negativity.

Tell yourself that "you're going to enjoy all the bullsh-- you have to deal with as you chase your goals and dreams, because you want to remember them all," Cuban advises. "Each and every experience will serve as motivation and provide great memories when you finally make it all happen."

Business Lesson

Our attitude and approach to life can be pivotal to our happiness. By waking up ready to take on the day, and retaining a sense of hope and possibility, we're setting ourselves up for success. On the flip side, anxiously awaiting the day's challenges, stressing about our schedule, and focusing on the negative will position us for the opposite. In addition, once we choose to take on a certain outlook, it has the tendency to become a constant in our lives, impacting our perspective and changing how we approach even the smallest challenge.

Some individuals seem to be innately optimistic, however it's not something that is unchangeable.

Rather, it's an approach that we are able to control. As each day begins, we can choose to tackle the day with positivity, or decide to assume the worst. Studies show us that over time, having an optimistic attitude equips us to deal with stress, stay healthier, live longer, and ultimately lead happier lives than being pessimistic.

Thankfully, optimism can be improved, and here are some ways to raise the bar:

- **Discover the silver lining.** An optimist is someone who focuses on the positive of any situation. In the case of a car accident, an optimist might focus on the fact that nobody was badly hurt and it's simply a matter of filing an insurance claim and getting the car repaired. It doesn't mean the situation or the problem is being ignored. However, an optimist knows that bad situations will inevitably happen, and although frustrating, they are temporary challenges that can be overcome.

- **Surround yourself with positivity.** The friends and colleagues you surround yourself with can be a key factor in the outlook you take on. Being around pessimistic people all the time can lead you to have a very negative demeanor. By making an effort to avoid negativity whenever possible and surround yourself with positive, supportive people, you can improve your outlook as well.

- **Be realistic about life's twists and turns.** Being realistic allows us to avoid blowing a situation out of proportion. As an optimist, there will undoubtedly be negative situations and rough days--it's part of life. Nobody can be positive all of the time; however, by realizing there will be ups and downs, successes and setbacks, it allows us to be more resilient when hard times present themselves.

- **Understand that everything is temporary.** Studies indicate that optimists and pessimists interpret the drivers of success or failure in a different way. Pessimists have a tendency to see events as permanent, impacting their lives significantly, whereas optimists realize struggles are temporary. Pessimists may take things very personally, whereas optimists see adversity as something that is simply happening, rather than happening *to them*. Pessimists also have a tendency to overestimate the extent to which one issue will permeate other areas of their life, while optimists may have an easier time taking challenges in stride.

Quote #13

"Everyone has ideas, most don't do the work required to get the job done."

Quote Meaning

"Everyone has ideas, most don't do the work required to get the job done," Mark Cuban stated once in a Q&A session on Reddit. He was answering the question posed to him about what entrepreneurs need to understand when launching a business.

Cuban has frequently offered the controversial advice for entrepreneurs to skip business school. "I think an MBA is an absolute waste of money," he wrote on Reddit, "I don't give any advantage to someone in hiring because they have an MBA." In place of a graduate degree in business, Cuban suggests bolstering your knowledge with free courses that can be found online.

Many people have had a business idea in the back of their mind for months or even years. Often, people will wait an exceptionally long period of time before jumping into action. Some individuals are focused on their full time job and haven't found the time to launch a new business; others have a family or other responsibilities that hold them back from taking the leap. Perhaps some people question their ability to accomplish their dream, or may lack the tools or knowledge to take the next step.

The issue lies in the space between having the idea and taking action to achieve it. As Cuban states, it's extremely easy to get excited by a brilliant idea or an exciting dream, but it's another thing to take the plunge and put your concept into action.

Business Lesson

If you've ever sat on a great idea, thinking about doing it, but failing to take action, you're not alone. Unfortunately, most times this means your idea will simply die. Countless business ideas have gone nowhere because of a person's inability to act. Many people have great ideas, but either due to fear, lack of time or countless other reasons, they fail to move forward. They may plan to eventually act on their ideas, but when the time finally comes, their concept doesn't make sense anymore, or has been put into action by someone else.

However, there are ways to tackle inaction.

- **Don't Let Your Ideas Die:** As business people constantly taking in new information and learning from others, most of us are continuously generating new ideas. However, to ensure our great ideas don't just fade into the abyss, we must also take action.

- **Write It Down:** When you're struck with an idea, the first step is to write it or record it somewhere. An easy solution is to use the Evernote app to record ideas. Evernote lets you save ideas from your desktop or laptop, whatever you prefer. With the ability to geotag the location, or add photos, videos and audio, you'll always be able to remember the context behind your idea.

The important thing is simply ensuring the ideas are recorded. If Evernote isn't your style, figure out a different way to keep track:

- o Notebook
- o Sticky note
- o Note app
- o Writing on a whiteboard
- o Sending an email to yourself
- o Leaving a voicemail for yourself

Whatever is most convenient for you will be the most sustainable way of recording your ideas. With it written down, you can return to your idea later, when you're ready to take action.

- **Do Something:** It's important to revisit your ideas every so often. Even if they've been written down, if they are never acted on, they will eventually become irrelevant or unoriginal. Make an effort to return to your ideas regularly and then do something to act on them.

It doesn't have to be big - if you have a great concept for a blog post, begin a draft. If it's an art piece, start sketching. Instead of worrying about finishing the project, getting it perfect or sharing it with others, simply get started. Even a step in the right direction is better than nothing.

- **Just Ship It:** Often, we have a tendency to take way too long to finish something, especially those who struggle with perfectionism. Stressing about getting something perfect can stifle and kill creativity. Instead of waiting for perfection, push yourself to put something out that isn't quite finished. There's always the chance to revisit the concept and revise. Don't sacrifice taking action by waiting for elusive perfection, and just get it shipped. Taking action is pivotal in achieving success. Inaction is the enemy of creativity, momentum and results.

Quote #14

"Do Something Different"

Quote Meaning

Mark Cuban once said, "When you've got 10,000 people trying to do the same thing, why would you want to be number 10,001?"

In his role as an angel investor, Cuban is constantly on the hunt for companies that can indicate exactly what makes them different. In fact, if companies aren't clear about their niche, he doesn't waste any time. "Wherever I see people doing something the way it's always been done, the way it's 'supposed' to be done, following the same old trends, well, that's just a big red flag to me to go look somewhere else."

For those who prefer to do what's always been done and follow through with tried-and-true methods, there's always the option to open a franchise. However, entrepreneurs seeking the kind of success that Cuban has accomplished need to be completely different. It's definitely a minority of people who are willing to push the boundaries and try something completely different and unexpected. However, it's also a major reason why these people tend to achieve great things. It ultimately comes back to the cliché stating that doing what *most* people are doing will earn you the same accomplishments as *most* people.

Most entrepreneurs would agree they don't want to end up as another statistic. With the amount of marriages that lead to divorce, or the number of people plagued with depression, living a "typical" existence is not something you want to aspire to. Instead, revel in the "different". While others may criticize you or question your decisions, others will envy you for having the courage to stand out from the crowd.

Ultimately, don't fear being different--and remember that the most successful people in history had to adjust to being an outlier, rather than a follower.

Business Lesson

We know that if we don't stand out from the competition, we can't expect to earn more than our competitors either. In addition, we know that what makes us "different" has to be appropriately communicated to the customer in order to win their business. Consequently, the challenge facing most business owners is being able to separate themselves from others and be able to demand a higher price for what they offer.

Here are a number of simple, actionable ways you can ensure you're standing out from the rest:

Begin With You. Most business owners are much better than they realize. Nobody can sell your services better than you. Think about how you can ask your clients more unique and insightful questions. Spend time getting to the root of their problems and being proactive in your approach. Finally, let your passion and personality come through in every interaction. If you love what you do, it should show in your work.

Be Solutions-Focused. You may have already heard that customers don't care about your services, but the problem you're solving. Glossy ads and marketing brochures are not going to win over your customers. Instead, look at the world through their perspective and figure out exactly what you need to do to fix their pain points.

Show Your Client A Different Way. Often, customers can start the process with their own ideas and a pre-set expectation of how to solve the problem. By focusing on your unique skill set and how YOU can solve the customer's problem, you can guide them to a solution they may not have considered. Don't be afraid to suggest a new approach or a unique way of addressing the issues at hand.

You Are An Investment, Not A Cost. Redefining your services as an investment, rather than a "purchase" will greatly improve your relationship with the customer. By walking a customer through the process of "investing," rather than "purchasing," our whole perspective changes. Rather than focusing in on the specific features of what we sell, we can zero in on how to generate a return on investment for the client.

Understand The Beneficiaries Of Your Service. During a pitch, many people will focus on getting the decision maker to say "yes" to what they're offering. However in many cases, the person making the decision is not the beneficiary of your service. By focusing on the people who will truly benefit from what you're offering, your proposal will be much more valuable.

Avoid Comparisons. If you truly believe your product or service is different, it doesn't make sense to make comparisons. What you offer is truly incomparable, so while many salespeople may employ this tactic, it's wise to avoid it.

All these tips are clear, actionable items you can implement immediately. By differentiating yourself and communicating your unique value to potential customers, you'll have the ability to demand higher compensation and carve out your reputation as a leader in your industry.

Quote #15

"Know Your Business Better than Anyone"

Quote Meaning

Cuban has often stated, "You got to be the smartest guy in the room about your product." In fact, he's known to invest so much time researching his industries that he told TechCrunch, "I need a break because I spend so much time reading. If there's something I get into, I won't stop. I read a lot of industry trade publications for cable now."

Cuban believes that, in order to create a successful company, the more knowledge you equip yourself with, the better. His advice is straightforward, yet often difficult to implement: "Know your business and industry better than anyone else in the world."

If you want to be able to beat your competition and stand out from the crowd, you need to be an absolute expert in your industry. Arm yourself with the information, resources, and knowledge, and commit to continuously learn more about your craft.

Business Lesson

One of the primary reasons business owners fail is lacking knowledge in their own industry. In order to succeed, you require unparalleled knowledge of the subject matter and a deep understanding of the problems your potential customers are facing.

Taking the time to intricately understand your industry will allow you to get a leg up over your competitors. At a minimum, the following areas should be thoroughly considered:

- **How Profit is Made.** Firstly, take an objective look into how profit is made in your industry. How are your competitors making a profit? While this may seem obvious, many entrepreneurs never take the time to ask this question. However, it's one of the most important things to consider--if it's not profitable, your business will not succeed. *Knowing* how to bring in money is key, and a great starting point is understanding what your competitors are doing to make a profit.

- **Expenses.** Analyze all the expenses that come with operating a business in your industry. From startup costs, purchasing overhead, or logistics.

- **Consider the Logistics Chain.** Consider whether there will be any potential logistical issues with your business. Look objectively at the process of purchasing your products and how you ship them to customers. If you're struggling with logistical issues after a client places an order, the customer experience is going to be negatively impacted. Being prepared is key in refining your logistical process. Consider potential obstacles and envision the entire shipping process to prepare for any issues.

- **What Do Your Customers Want?** If you don't have a clear understanding of who your target market is, you'll never be able to address their specific needs. The only way to know your target market is through research. Start by gaining a deep understanding of their biggest fears and pain points. If you're going to sell a product or service that helps them, you need to have a strong grasp on how they think and behave. Narrow down your target market by demographic and psychographic--then, create customer personas so you can continuously remind yourself who your target is.

- **Competitor Analysis.** It's absolutely essential that you analyze your competitors. Know exactly how much they're pulling in for profit. Identify how they gain customers. Consider their logistics and know where you stand. Analyzing your competitors has great value--not only does it provide you an idea of how to run your own business, but it also allows you to capitalize on any issues or weaknesses they may have. Imagine your main competitor is faced with a logistics problem pertaining to product delivery. Perhaps it takes them 60 minutes to deliver, yet your company can deliver in 40 minutes. This could then serve as a unique selling proposition (USP) for your own business.

- **Understand Your Industry.** Before anything, you need to have a deep understanding of your particular industry. While knowing your target market, completing a competitor analysis, and addressing weaknesses are all important factors, you can explore even further. Consider the current economy and what kind of impact this may have on businesses in your sector. Consider whether your industry exhibits high growth or slow growth. Think about potential opportunities for long-term profit or sustainability. Consider how many companies are already in operation, and the types of products or services they offer. Pay close attention to cyclical or seasonal changes that may have an impact on sales. Consider customers in the industry. How often do they buy? Do they buy infrequently, or on a regular basis? Brainstorm potential legal issues that could crop up when starting a business in your sector. Is there an ideal business structure? What are your legal obligations? By undertaking a thorough industry analysis, you'll be well equipped to deal with the twists and turns that every business owner faces on the road to success.

By now, you undoubtedly realize the importance of knowing your industry, and the insight this research can provide into the profitability and sustainability of your business. Knowing your industry well is a great first step that will ultimately save you effort, time and expense down the road.

Conclusion

Thank you for purchasing this book and reading it this far. I hope you have learned something that is considered valuable from Mark Cuban.

Finally, if you enjoyed this book, then I'd like to ask you for a favor, would you be kind enough to leave a review for this book on Amazon? Tell us what you like or dislike and what we can improve. Your feedbacks will be greatly appreciated!

https://www.amazon.com/dp/B01M7MHGLF

Also follow EntrepreneurshipFacts on social media to stay updated with our new books and increase your knowledge about business and successful people on a daily basis:

Instagram   Facebook   Twitter

Check out our website for the latest facts and articles about business and entrepreneurship:

www.EntrepreneurshipFacts.com

Do you want to know more about Mark Cuban?

Check out our book:

https://www.amazon.com/dp/B01N47NUZL

MARK CUBAN - The Life & Success Stories Of A Shark Billionaire: Biography

SPECIAL OFFER!!! Get the paperback version and receive the kindle ebook version ($2.99) for FREE!!!

More books by Entrepreneurship Facts

101 Entrepreneurial Facts About 10 of The Most Successful BILLIONAIRES That Can Inspire You: What you can learn from their successes

101 Fascinating Facts About 10 Of The Most Recognizable Companies In The World

The Real Life RICH DAD & The Lessons He Taught ROBERT KIYOSAKI about Money

Warren Buffett - 41 Fascinating Facts about Life & Investing Philosophy: The Lessons From A Legendary Investor

Elon Musk - Top 10 Business Lessons Through An Inspiring Life Of A Visionary Entrepreneur:

DONALD TRUMP - Top 5 Business Lessons From The Presidential Campaign Of A Businessman: The Art Of Getting Attention

Richard Branson - Top 13 Secrets To Success in Life & Business: A Virgin Entrepreneur

Steve Jobs - Top 13 Secrets To Success in Life & Business: The Power Of Think Different

Printed in Great Britain
by Amazon